D1242234

Schools Council Art and Craft Education
8 to 13 Project

USING   NATURAL   MATERIALS

Schools Council Art and Craft Education
8 to 13 Project

Seonaid Robertson

USING NATURAL MATERIALS

VAN NOSTRAND REINHOLD COMPANY
New York · Cincinnati · Toronto · London · Melbourne

ACKNOWLEDGEMENTS

I would like to thank Ann Goodwin, Jeff Lowe, Mary Seyd, and Pennsylvania State University for permission to reproduce the colour photographs on pages 26, 27, 34 and 35.

Van Nostrand Reinhold Company Regional Offices:
New York   Cincinnati   Chicago   Millbrae   Dallas

Van Nostrand Reinhold Company International Offices:
London   Toronto   Melbourne

Copyright © Schools Council Publications 1974
Library of Congress Catalog Card Number 73 14359
ISBN 0 442 29998 2

Printed in Great Britain by Jolly and Barber Ltd., Rugby and bound by the Ferndale Book Company.

Designed by Rod Josey.

Published by Van Nostrand Reinhold Company, 450 West 33rd St., New York, N.Y. 10001, and Van Nostrand Reinhold Company Ltd., 25–28 Buckingham Gate, London SW1E 6LQ.

16 15 14 13 12 11 10 9 8 7 6 5 4 3 2 1

Library of Congress Cataloging in Publication Data

Robertson, Seonaid Mairi.
  Using natural materials.

  1. Preceptual learning.   2. Nature study.
3. Creative thinking (Education).   I. Title.
LB1067.R58   372.3′57   73-14359
ISBN 0-442-29998-2

Contents

Introduction

NATURAL MATERIALS

All materials might be described as being originally natural, since our only source of material is the earth, its seas and the atmosphere surrounding it, but many products which we use in life and in the art lesson have gone through so many processes that they carry no hint, no smell, no feel of the raw material that was their source. These products form the major part of every child's experiences; the linoleum on the kitchen floor, the plastic bowl for washing up, the drip-dry fabrics which, by easing washing day, should enable him to get dirty without fuss.

Our only source of materials (photo Australian News and Information Bureau).

NASA ATS III MSSCC 18 NOV 67 153255Z SSP 49.16°W 0.03°S ALT 22240.59 SM

Many children who grow up in cities have almost no contact with any living or growing thing and it is for this reason that we should offer these children as many opportunities for handling natural materials as possible. If we do this we shall not only widen their experience enormously but present to them an infinite variety which custom cannot stale.

We owe children opportunities for handling natural things (photo Geoff Newman).

A boy arranging his collection of pebbles in a garden (photo Geoff Newman).

Traditional straw decorations
(photo Ann Goodwin).

Straw fan decoration for a
party or a festival (photo
Ann Goodwin).

For country children the world and materials of nature are an accepted heritage and one that is sometimes too casually acknowledged. The country schools could and should be living museums of skills, both of the traditional types that can be learnt from grandfathers and of those still in use that can be learnt from regional craftsmen. They should open up new ways of using local materials in the contemporary world. Straw harvest dolls (see page 26) may have lost their ancient symbolism, although it can be interesting to discover their previous significance, but they are fun to make as Christmas decorations, and the traditional containers made of straw, withy and wood, still find a welcome place in modern homes. Everyone would be the poorer if these activities died out, for many cannot be learnt from books but only from practitioners of each craft. This is also a natural and pleasurable way to bring together children and adults.

Traditional straw containers
for logs – lightweight and
flexible (photo COSIRA).

There are many ways in which city children can be given the chance to handle natural materials. This may occur on a camping holiday, a weekend's excursion or a day-trip, but when planning this type of excursion children will gain more if they have been prepared and helped to look at and handle the natural materials they will find, rather than being presented with questionnaires or asked to write reports. With tact and enthusiasm, adults will enable children to experience the pleasure of discovering and handling materials for themselves, which will make this much more meaningful.

However, discovering natural materials even for those who live in the city, need not depend on organized trips to the countryside or seashore. Many materials can be searched for and found in city waste and even grown in window boxes and tubs. Some schools have enlisted the help of fathers to dig up a part of a barren playground to start a garden and if the children are involved in this they will be able to take part in building, transporting, begging or buying soil, the ordering of seeds and making records of everything planted and grown. This is education in the most natural way possible, making direct contact with the world outside school.

Enjoying the bodily freedom and exercise which the countryside offers all children (photo Geoff Newman).

Even if a garden is an impractical proposition, any school can provide window boxes and small plant containers. These are sufficient to grow plants for dyeing and herbs for cooking. They will also attract insects and butterflies which can encourage the habit of close observation – leading children to explore the world beyond the confines of the classroom.

If youngsters in cities and towns have been educated in this way and encouraged to seek out and find things for themselves, if they have been encouraged to bring to school their own treasures and finds from the waste of over-prodigal cities, then they will not have to be urged to bring home from an excursion the sticks, stones and shells, bleached bones and wood that take their fancy. These personal objects can be displayed in the school, or carried and handled for a while in the pocket where they will form a continuing and personal link with the countryside. They will act as a witness to its continuing existence, waiting to be rediscovered whenever we care to go and look for it.

The smooth surfaces of pebbles (photo Mary Seyd).

The touch and smell of shells and bones brought home from excursions remind us of a wider world (photo Geoff Newman).

A child who has never seen that shy animal, the badger, explores its skull by sight and touch (photo Geoff Newman).

If children who live in cities are initiated into the countryside in this way in the company of one who cares deeply for it, they may well be led to an attitude of caring, and to the desire to conserve both living things and the organic communities which embody so much of our history, for the enjoyment of generations to come. This attitude is engendered through caring for plants and pets (see page 27); one feather from a bird may start a long flight of thought in a child. The 'subject' a teacher professes is far less important than the attitude to life he unconsciously conveys.

Caring for living things which they have grown themselves leads children to an appreciation of the individual nature and qualities of each different plant (photo Geoff Newman).

Caring for animals develops protective instincts in boys and girls (photo Geoff Newman).

A feather reveals its intricate growth (photo Mary Seyd).

13

Chapter 1

LOOKING, SEARCHING

A city street (photo Picturepoint).

Seeing is one of the basic ways in which children get to know the world in which they are growing up. Learning to identify visual shapes is part of an essential knowledge of our environment. We all see the same buildings, vehicles, pavements and railings, but how few of us get any positive visual pleasure from these sights (see page 27). It is a sad depreciation of life if observing becomes a purely functional process enabling us to steer our way through the complexity of a city street. All teachers can help children *look* at what they *see*.

A country lane (photo J. Allan Cash).

Country children and, in particular, city children, need to be led into observing the natural world, which surrounds them and to which they can turn for refreshment and recreation, by some knowledge of the structure and purpose of natural things.

Trees silhouetted against the sky (photo Geoff Newman).

The death of this forest giant will provide the raw material for our furniture and boats.

A traditional rush seated chair (photo COSIRA).

An awareness of the ways in which different trees grow, each identifiable from one fallen leaf, or of the extraordinary variety of insects, the ladybird, the frail-fierce dragonfly, the furry evening moth, can add immensely to the interest of countryside or garden. Children should also learn about the nature of the plants they see growing.

Many of us have to live in cities, but the country offers different contours and different textures:
The winter skeletons of trees reveal the variety of their growth (photo J. Allan Cash).

The frail-fierce dragonfly (photo S. C. Bisserot and Bruce Colman Ltd.).

The furry evening moth (photo S. C. Bisserot and Bruce Colman Ltd.).

Those who pick the Ryvita from the almost identical Vitawheat packet for their mothers in the supermarket, have the right to know the distinctive heads of rye, barley, wheat and oats. They can learn about the variety of grasses and the part these play in the food chain for the horses, cows and sheep they see grazing in the fields.

Children have a right to know the distinctive heads of rye, barley, wheat and oats (photos John Topham Ltd.).

Grass heads (photo Mary Seyd).

The feathery heads of grasses (photo Francis McNally).

Collecting every wild flower found is fun, but when one wants to distinguish between ladies' bedstraw and woodruff, tansy and ragwort, in order to make dyes from them, it is necessary to develop a more acute observation (see page 27). The use of a magnifying glass for a grasshead or an insect, a microscope for a crystal or a snowflake, will add a new dimension to the world of nature.

A magnified crystal can add a new dimension to the world of nature (photo Glaxo Laboratories Ltd.).

The veins of a leaf support the structure and carry the nutrients of the earth to its outer edges (photo Mary Seyd).

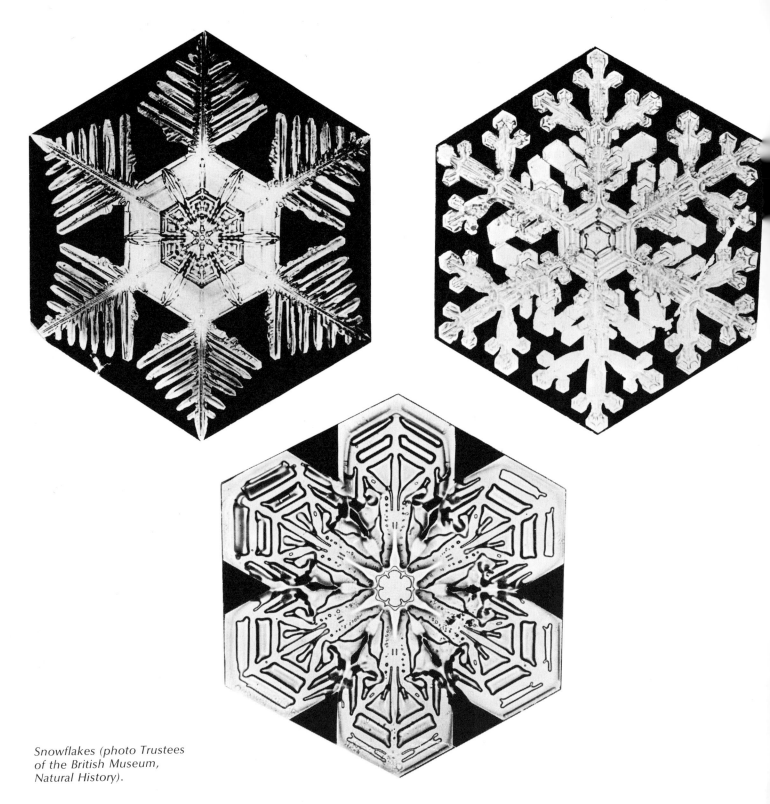

Snowflakes (photo Trustees of the British Museum, Natural History).

Primary school children rediscovering a traditional craft in the plaiting of straw dollies.

A straw bonnet and a crown, developed from traditional straw dollies.

Top right. Children may move from an enjoyment of cuddly animals to an interest in more unusual pets, such as hedgehogs or grass snakes.

Bottom right. Golden-rod for dyes.

Stones skilfully fitted together by a wall builder.

Above. Clay accepts the slightest impulse of the fingers.

Arranging leaves within a given space may bring home to a child their immense variety and ways of growth.

27

*A landscape transformed by
snow (photo Mary Seyd).*

Children's senses can be heightened by simple exercises in judgement; arranging a collection of stones in a series from blackest to whitest, or of barks from softest to hardest by touch, or distinguishing blindfold between leaf textures from smoothest to woolliest. If they find any series incomplete the children can be encouraged to go out and try to find the material to complete it. This is an ideal occupation for those moments when children feel at a loss with more 'creative' work; looking at and handling things which have a natural vitality often stir the creative impulse.

A collection of shells from the seashore (photo Geoff Newman).

A schoolgirl gathering wool from a barbed-wire fence (photo Geoff Newman).

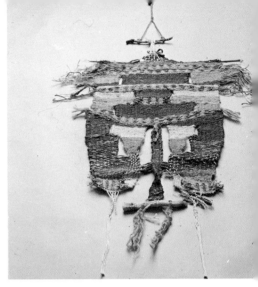

Top left. Jewellery of bone, nuts and seeds strung on wire by children.

Top centre. Privet, onions, lombardy poplar and bark with hanks of wool dyed from them.

Top right. A first weaving on a home-made loom incorporating rushes and wool dyed with lichen and onion.

Left. Necklace of oak-apples made by a child.

Bottom left. Sand sculpture by children.

Bottom right. This kiln has an inner chamber of four kiln shelves plastered together with rough clay. It is shown packed ready for the first or biscuit firing on wood stacked round as fuel.

The satisfaction of the comic in clay.

Building the structure of a simple sawdust kiln.

Children must learn to control fire.

Teazing wool before spinning.

A group of 10 year-old children in Wiltshire went out to look at their chalky environment. They noticed the rounded hills, the lack of streams, the siting of the buildings of flint and thatch. They gathered wool ends from the fences and, having made their own spindles of baked clay similar to those of 6,000 years ago, they tried the ancient art of spinning.

Carding to 'comb' the fibres and make them lie parallel.

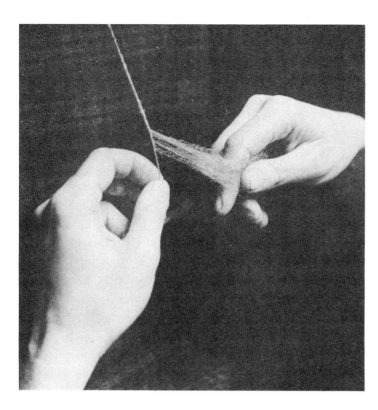

Hands in spinning are
sensitive to the tug of the
wool.

The next 'tail' for spinning is
ready on her knee.

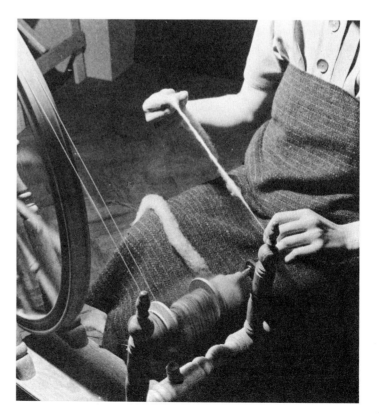

Above. Carving into the wood with a chisel.

Far left. Papermaking: Lifting a corner of the paper from the mould.

Gently peeling the paper off.

Looking at the texture of a thick hand-made paper.

Left. Children can bring back a log from a camping holiday and carve it into a totem pole in the garden.

Woven hanging made without a loom from plant dyed fibres, reeds and grasses.

A sculpture making use of the grain of the wood.

A child's work with hedgerow material (photo Jeff Lowe).

Below right:
Sheep hurdles of wattle are light, pliable and serve for protection at lambing time (photo COSIRA).

36

With the raw, pliable twigs and branches they collected and long strands of bindwood from the hedges, they made an assortment of baskets and mats. Then, under their teacher's guidance, they tried their hands at making sheep wattles and at thatching a little wooden hut, recreating the occupations of their rural forebears and neighbours. They rediscovered some of the ways in which man has used what lay around him for the basic needs of enclosure and shelter, for carrying produce and keeping warm. In this way children can learn to understand the complexity of simple tasks, they no longer take 'home' for granted.

Traditional thatching (photo COSIRA).

A witch doctor's mask of wattle and straw made by a child (photo Jeff Lowe).

Chapter 2

FINDING, CHOOSING

We do not all respond to the same materials, and the more timid of us need encouragement to try something unfamiliar. However, there is such a variety of free and interesting material available for collecting that there is no excuse for limiting a whole group of children to working in one material for too long.

When introduced to natural materials each child's response is entirely individual. Clay is an essential medium for all young children, accepting the slightest impulse of the fingers and holding it in a permanent form (see page 27).

*Child finding clay (photo
Geoff Newman).*

Preparing clay brought in
from the countryside.

The enjoyment of pounding
clay.

Children who have not used clay at a young age may reject it in early adolescence, but they may respond to resistant materials which challenge, or to delicate things such as silk, thread, dried honesty-capsules, seeds, spider webs, which inspire fine constructions. Some love the rough and silky textures of wool and learn to discriminate between them as finely as a musician's ear discriminates between tones. Others respond to the hard precision of stone or metal, or to the fragility of a bird's skeleton.

A teacher's encouragement of the child to make a selection of materials that attract him implies a respect for the child and of his capability of making a choice. *A material to which an individual has sensuously and intuitively responded offers not only a source of inspiration but its own inherent discipline.* In the act of decision-making and in the continued living with his choice (considering how the original response may change or deepen) each individual, adult or child, is becoming more completely himself, reinforcing his personality.

Seeds float like tiny parachutes (photo Mary Seyd).

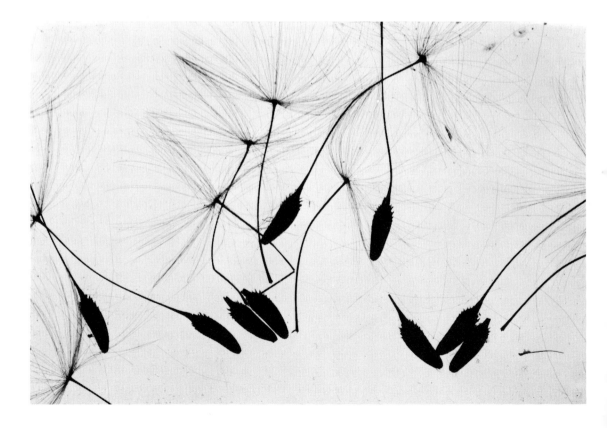

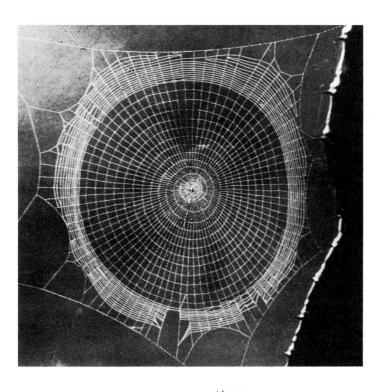

Below:
The hard precision of stone.

Above:
'The points of leaves and twigs on which the spider begins her work are few, and she fills the air with a beautiful circuiting' – Keats to his friend Reynolds (photo Trustees of the British Museum, Natural History).

We gravitate to our friends' bookshelves, pin-up displays or collections of objects, and in learning what they value and choose to live with, we discover new facets of their personalities. Similarly our own collections can reinforce our sense of ourselves. We are all more or less sentimental about objects, but if the objects have intrinsic qualities of their own, *we* will grow through continued association with them, as we do through a relationship with interesting people.

We adults, who have so many possessions, often forget how much a few objects may mean to a child. Before school age most 'toys' are manufactured objects given by well meaning adults. As the child gets older, treasures may then be found among the throw-outs of the adult world, and perhaps in adolescence mirror a rejection of its values. So, children in this 8 to 13 age group often develop a mania for collecting, and can be encouraged to build up their own little collections of

Left and right:
A nautilus shell – the more permanent structure of a sea creature (photo Francis McNally).

shells, pebbles, plants, fossils. Fortunately these seldom become money-status symbols, but are treasured for themselves. Their value is extended by the children sharing their enjoyment with each other, and by leading them to talking about, explaining, finding out about the objects they have assembled. The collections may be the inspiration for embroidery or painting and may also lead the children into the related fields of geology, geography, biology, history. For the natural forms that cannot be collected, such as spiders' webs, the children can be encouraged to make carefully observed drawings or to take photographs. Many young children now have cameras and for them building up a record of such transient sights may lead to the discovery of photography as an art in itself.

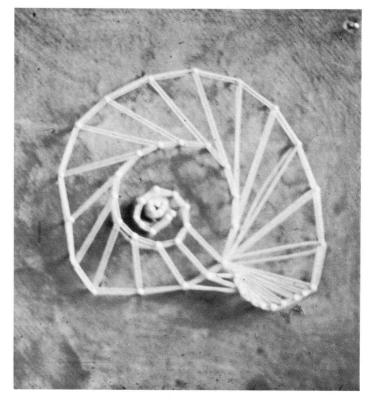

Fossils found far inland remind us that much of our countryside was once under the sea (photo Geoff Newman).

A child's drawing in string and thread of one shell from a collection.

Chapter 3

APPRECIATING, SHARING

Some of the things we value may be such intimate and personal treasures that they are carried in the pocket or hidden from casual eyes. Many, however, need to be isolated and displayed (see page 27) so that they can be seen free of the clutter of daily living. My introduction to working with natural materials for those children and adults who have been unfortunate enough to miss rural experiences is to bring in a car-load full of 'loot' from the countryside – stones, pebbles, bark, leaves, plants in bud or seedpod – and spread them round the periphery of the working area to allow for free movement. A few simple containers, clay or Plasticine to 'bed' stems, and some wire, adhesive and thread are the only additional materials needed. I then suggest that each one spends time going round to find something to which he responds and takes it away to his corner. He must find a way of emphasizing for other people the colour, shape, fragility, humour, some aspect of the object he values.

There are many ways of doing this. Two objects may be put together in order to underline their qualities by similarity or contrast. Older children might use spotlights to do this, or display interesting shapes in 'view-boxes'. Corridors of boxes can be built for such displays, with carefully chosen background material and a fixed angle through which to peer. Children can discover tactile qualities through covered 'feelie-boxes', with circular holes through which, undisturbed by sight, they put their hands and enjoy texture and shape.

Isolating a single leaf brings out its individual pattern (photo Francis McNally).

44

Arranging leaves within a given space may bring home to a child their immense variety and ways of growth.

Using a 'feelie box' (photo Geoff Newman).

At the same time display should not be over-emphasized for children of this age. In a laudable attempt to avoid tatty pin-ups and to raise standards, display has become a fetish in some of our good primary schools, where a child can hardly dare pin his own work casually on the wall to assess or admire it. The classroom is also a workroom and long-term displays should be limited to one part of it. Otherwise it becomes a museum rather than a living, changing workshop. Teachers can encourage children to be uninhibited about displaying their treasures by bringing in their own objects and displaying them in some appropriate way. It is very satisfying when the children come and put their finds alongside our own.

This appreciation of found objects may result in children wishing to *emphasize* and *enhance* their qualities. This boy (see illus.) has chosen his favourite pebbles and polished them in a simple electric grinder for many hours. From time to time he has taken them out to handle them fondly and decide whether they would benefit from more polishing, whether they should be kept to handle and admire or be set in some way. For him every yard of a walk by a river-bed or on a beach will hold interest from now on.

Below, right :
A local church may well provide the chance to see the solemn or comic stone carvings of earlier centuries, such as this one from Hexham Abbey.

Choosing pebbles to put through an electric grinder (photo Bill Darrell).

Appreciation of what they see can also lead children back in time. A visit to a church with Romanesque carvings, to a Celtic cross or an 18th century graveyard, to a museum or archaeological excavation, even browsing in a book of prehistoric, early Mediterranean or pre-Columbian illustrations, will open up some of the great traditions of art to which a child might find his own work naturally akin.

Constantly changing books and illustrations on the walls, far from encouraging pseudo-primitive styles, may provide material from which children can find confidence in their own work and can realise that the obsession with naturalism is a very recent and quite small part of the whole history of art.

The Celtic cross of Muiredach at Monasterboice, Ireland (photo Commissioners of Public Works in Ireland).

18th century gravestone (photo William Mann).

Chapter 4

ASSEMBLING, COMBINING

One of my ways of introducing materials has been to bring the natural world into the home, school or college for living decoration. Materials such as grasses, fibres, shells and nuts have interesting characteristics that encourage us to preserve and display them. Arranging flowers and branches, moss and stones, is a simple household form of display, while shells, nuts and seeds can be used to form appliqué pictures or be incorporated in stitchery. We can also draw with string, which, though it comes to us from manufacturers, retains enough of its fibre quality to be considered with natural materials. It can be unravelled, coiled, knotted, even built into the intricate constructions of knots called macramé, with its echoes of nets and rigging.

String and thread used to delineate a pea-pod (photo Mary Seyd).

String and thread used to delineate the interior of a fruit (photo Mary Seyd).

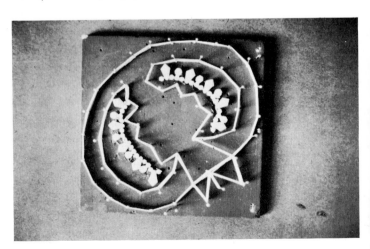

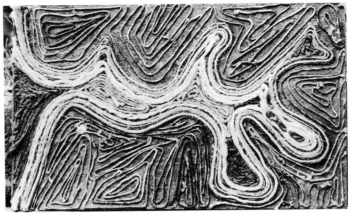

The inspiration of string, twine and thread (photo Mary Seyd).

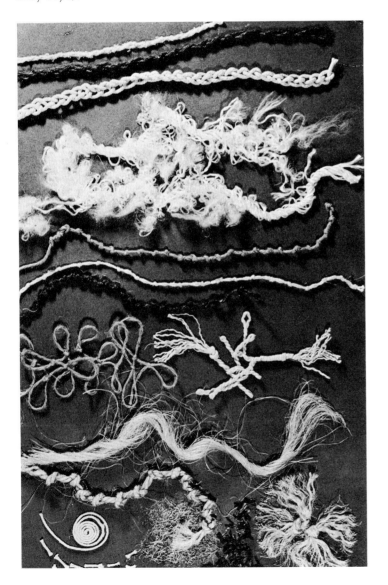

Mathematical patterns of string and pins.

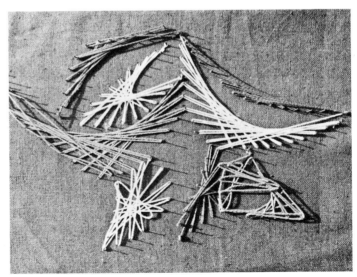

49

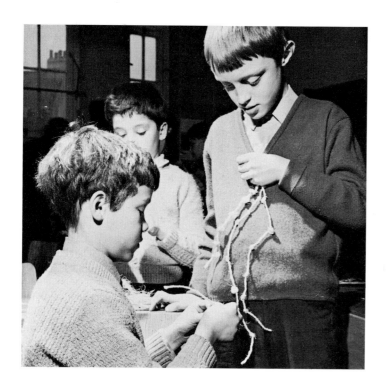

Boys knotting string as a preliminary to macramé (photo Art and Craft in Education).

Below, left:
A simple, practical use of string, traditional in the Orient (photo Geoff Newman).

A fisherman mending his net (photo COSIRA).

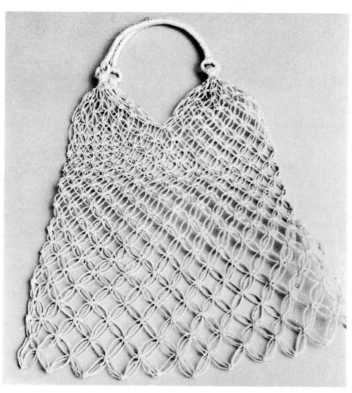

Seeds, nuts, bones suggest forms of self-adornment very attractive to this age group. Children can string them on nylon thread (see page 30) or fishing line, and from this move to work in wire with simple tools and on to copper and enamelled jewellery. Cones and shells can be sawn across revealing their structure, bored and strung on wire. This sort of question can be considered:

> Which type of seed for a bracelet?
> Which knuckle bones for a windchime?
> Which pattern of grouping to follow?
> How to make a fastener which does not scratch
>   the neck?

These all demand personal decisions, but a wrong choice will not be disastrous, so even a timid child can be daring.

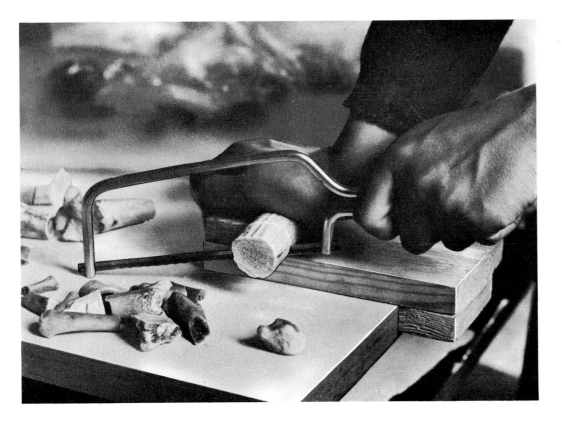

A boy sawing horn to make jewellery (photo Mary Seyd).

The waving tentacles of the
octopus in this shell collage
echo the creature's
movement through the sea
(photo Mary Seyd).

Shell collage panel on a
sand-texture background
(photo Mary Seyd).

Shells and pebbles can be brought back from a class or family excursion to the seashore, or collected from rivers. These can be handled by children as they consider their sources and shape:

> Stones now solid take us back to ages when the molten earth cooled, and we can trace the veins of red iron seeping along the cracks as the lava set. They are smooth or rubbed into irregular shapes by time.
>
> Shells are hollow, their surface texture is as symmetrical as the pattern of life of the creature whose home they were.

Rock pools can be made in old crocks, glass bowls, or perhaps in glass ovenware no longer in use. The durability of pebbles can be used to contribute in a more permanent form to our environment.

A rock pool with limpets (photo Mary Seyd).

Above and right:
*Shell and pebble mosaics
set by children in a public
patio.*

A class of children, in a middle school near the sea, used their studies and sketches of the seashore as the basis for a contribution to the neighbourhood. When a new terrace of flats was being built they enlarged their drawings to fill spaces of four square feet and set their pebble mosaics of fish, crabs, and an octopus in concrete. They prepared the stones, traced the drawing with pointed sticks, and laid the pieces in the wet concrete. How satisfying it was for the children to see these every time they passed and to know the appreciative response of the inhabitants of the houses. The children could not have achieved this without the friendly contacts, and the organisation of their teacher. This kind of teaching requires out-of-hours consultations and is not a nine to five job.

Every child should be capable of making something to be admired by parents and peers. Natural materials have their own qualities and therefore do not require great skill to produce an attractive result; the child co-operates with nature, revealing and relating its forms.

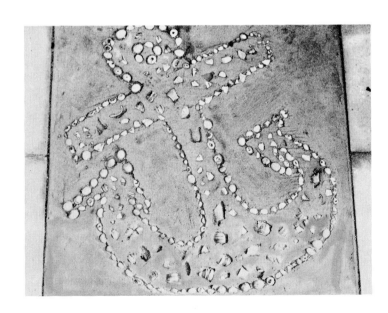

Above and left:
*Shell and pebble mosaics
set by children in a public
patio.*

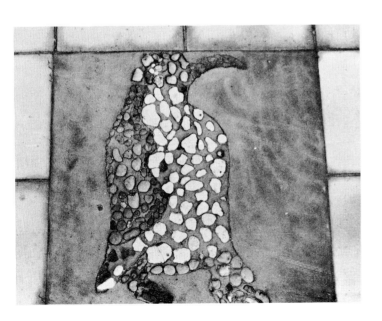

Chapter 5

REVEALING, SHAPING

Stones, nuts or seeds may be used just as they are without modification, as their shapes are clearly defined. Other materials, which can be found lying around or can be dug out with simple garden equipment, invite us to create our own forms. Clay is one of these, so responsive to the fingers that it has become an acknowledged craft material, whose importance in the middle school years cannot be over-emphasized.

City schools will obtain their clay in polythene bags and it is very important that it should be offered to children in the right plastic state or it will only be frustrating for them. Children can be taught how to keep it in good condition and to reconstitute it all the time. Clay that is too hard can be broken up in tiny pieces, laid on damp thick cloth or sacking and rolled into a 'roly-poly'. This will improve it in thirty minutes. If it is too damp it can be rolled and worked on a dry wood surface, or, better still, a plaster or fired clay bat, and it will be improved in about five minutes. The best introduction of all to clay, if the countryside is suitable, is for children to go and look for it along riverbeds or canals, to sieve and prepare it so that they understand that it is indeed the earth itself they are shaping.

Most parents, understandably, tend to provide clean materials for play, perhaps mass-produced pieces such as 'Lego', which can be gathered up quickly at mealtimes or bedtime. These toys have a value but are limited by the rigidity of the pieces and serve as an intellectual exercise rather than as an emotional outlet.

It is perhaps the primeval nature of clay that produces a crop of dragons.

For this reason it is now more than ever necessary to provide clay in schools. Many of the inexperienced teacher's problems can be avoided by introducing it outside when the weather is warm, because a bit of mess is part of the satisfaction of using clay. The children can be gradually taught to keep this under control, and to clean up after themselves. They should learn that cleaning up is part of life, part of the work cycle, and if they are given *time* to complete their work, not interrupted in the middle to clear away, they will do it cheerfully enough. Children from about 9 years upwards, when given the chance, will often work for a whole day or several days on end at a model or series of clayworks, and then, satisfied, turn to more formal work with equal enthusiasm.

Although looking at clay does not suggest images to them as do seeds, nuts, bones, most young children only need to get their hands into it to have ideas (see page 31). It is perhaps the primeval nature of the material that produces a crop of snakes and dragons. This can be extremely satisfying and is a phase that need not be hurried. Suggestions from the teacher about portraying the family or the family pet, or a favourite activity may lead on to work of increasing complexity.

When the children have had plenty of opportunity for individual work in clay, the teacher can initiate group work *for those who choose it,* suggesting that each one makes an animal or figure for Noah's Ark, or a Nativity, a bus queue or a team game. Children tend to identify their bodies with their models and turn the clay limbs this way and that until the position really represents the feeling. I have seen small children, when making a Nativity, 'walk on' their clay kings with their hands and press them down into a kneeling position. This type of group activity can also give immigrant children the opportunity to explain ceremonies and scenes from other cultures, such as a Hindu wedding, to other children in the class.

Group work: A near life-size figure in clay – Gulliver in Lilliputia.

This burnished clay object, fired in a sawdust kiln, is shaped to fit happily into a human hand.

Group work in which every child completes his own contribution and these are put together to make a larger whole, can lead on to collage or a joint embroidery or construction, where the parts have to be more closely integrated. This will involve children in discussion and criticism of each other's work, but although this is an educational and social progression, it should not be pressed on children. Art and craft is one of the school activities where each child can make his very personal product, and group work should go alongside and not be a substitute for this individual expressive work.

For young children the experience of shaping is of primary importance and clay is one of the few materials used in schools where the shape is completely within the child's control. At the same time clay is an accepted material in the adult world, being the raw material of artists and of industrial products used everywhere. The activity of modelling can go on all through life, developing imperceptibly into clay sculpture as a serious study. The spontaneous play of small children making model cups and teapots to be used in make-believe and abandoned, changes in the middle years into a desire to make more lasting vessels.

Decorating pots.

A clay bird on a nest.

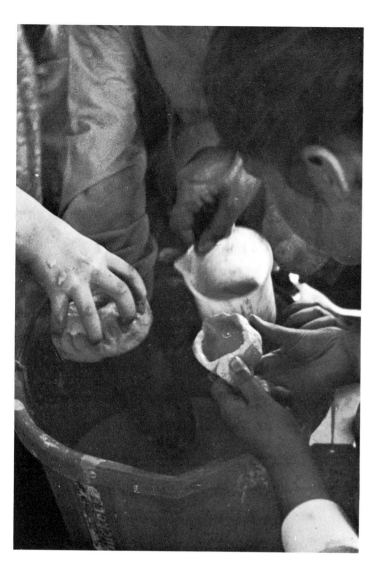

Dipping pots in glaze.

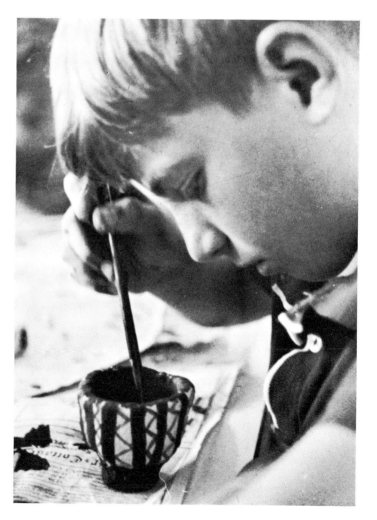

Decorating pots.

At this stage forms of hand shaping and slab building[1] can be introduced, and many small objects which do not require glazing can be made; containers for instance, plant pots for the classroom or home, nut and fruit dishes, tiles and slabs for heatproof stands (with felt later added to the bottom).[2] Kilns can be used, either the little classroom kilns that are available, or better still, the children can be given the opportunity to make their own, where they are more directly involved in the firing of their work (see page 30). Sawdust kilns, which cause no smoke and are safe to handle, can be built of old bricks in the playground or waste ground.

These primitive methods of firing can lead into discussion of early man and his technology, and from here to a visit to an archaeological site in the neighbourhood. On one occasion for example, a group of Londoners under inspiring leadership constructed Roman kilns after studying the archaeological remains in Highgate woods on the same site. On another, a number of families joined in a project at the Open Air Museum in Sussex (many of them camping) to reconstruct primitive kilns and investigate other basic technologies. Together children and parents can rediscover their country's history in a way they are not able to from books.

A child's drawing of a brick kiln with dustbin lid.

we made a sawdust kiln out of bricks we put pots in The kiln it is hot in the kiln

---

[1] There is a wonderful European tradition of clay dishes, decorated with slip of other colours, to be rediscovered by children, and American children can explore the colours used by the Indians, with the help of a series of booklets from the department of Indian Affairs.

[2] This is explored more thoroughly in *Creative Crafts in Education* by Seonaid Robertson, Routledge & Kegan Paul, 1952.

Building a sagger kiln outside a primary school.

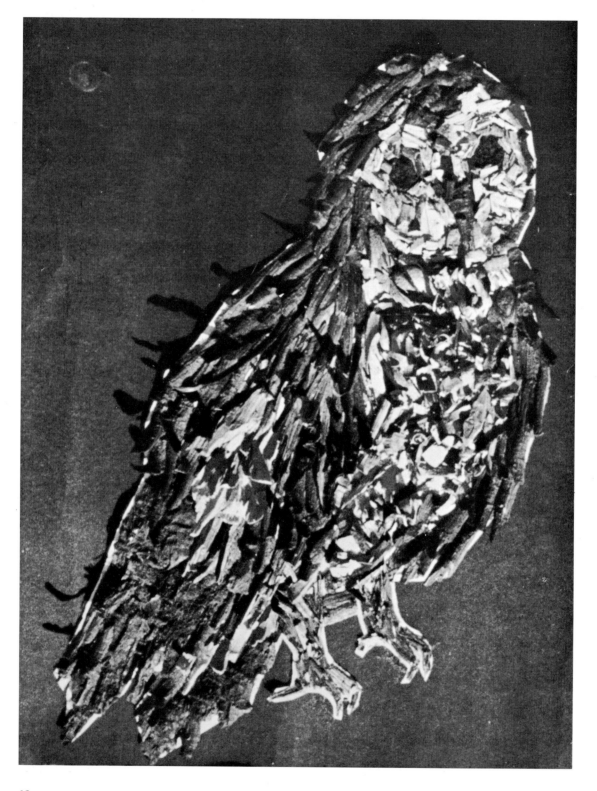

Owl made of bark and chip.
(photo Jeff Lowe).

Other hard materials should also be introduced in the middle years. Wood, 'clunch' and alabaster are natural materials which challenge children and yet can be carved with simple tools. Their distinctive qualities, variety of form and surface texture all help to suggest what can be made from them (see pages 34 and 35).

A landscape of bark and twigs (photo Jeff Lowe).

A mask of birch and straw (photo Jeff Lowe).

Below right:
A fantasy bird in wood shavings (photo Jeff Lowe).

For this totem pole, the boy has used the log, making little alteration to the original shape. Although he did not have the strength to transform the wood by carving, he used the contrast between the bark and the raw wood to indicate the features. Wood in a less 'natural' state can also be used. One young child has been led into handling it by combining offcuts to make figures. Other children used dowel rods to make a kite, applying their knowledge of mathematics and wind currents.

A simple totem pole using the contrast of bark and wood (photo Jeff Lowe).

Right:
*The result of a young
child playing with wood and
shavings (photo Jeff Lowe).*

Below:
Constructing a kite.

*Learning to use a brace
(photo Bill Darrell).*

*Tools for simple wood
gouging.*

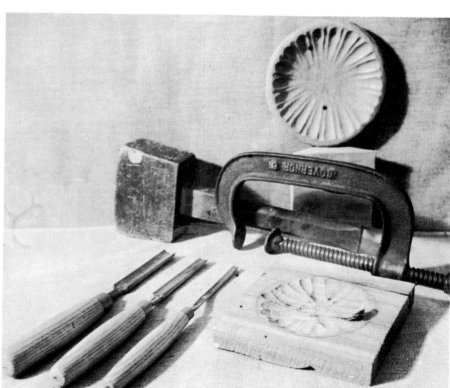

As children begin to use tools (see page 35) and learn to saw and bore, they may be led to more intricate objects. This painted eagle was traditional at riflemen's festivals in Germany and is now a feature at children's festivals there. Each part falls down separately when hit and the boy who shoots down the heart in the centre is 'king'. It was made from soft white wood decoratively painted, but children can learn to appreciate the qualities of wood better when handling a harder wood with its own subtle colours and graining.

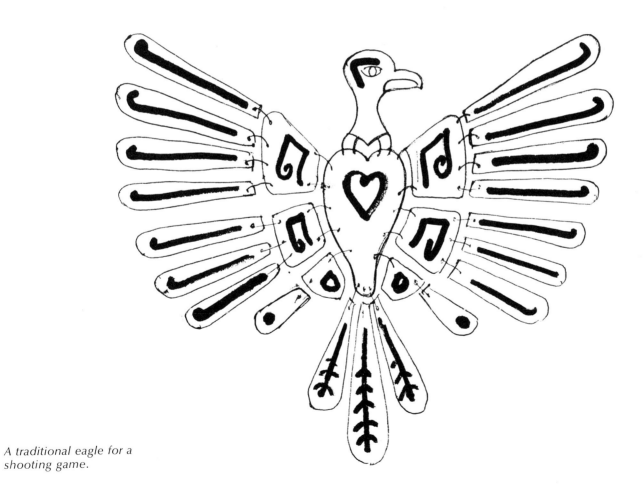

A traditional eagle for a shooting game.

Cooking spoons and a fruit dish made by gouging and a bird feeder made by turning (photo Geoff Newman).

The wood spoons and shallow bowls can be gouged with a minimum of equipment, and nut or fruit dishes are always acceptable items in the contemporary home. More elaborate tools are used by this 12 year-old boy repairing, with an electric sander, an old boat which he intends to use for in-shore excursions. The inspiration of one material may often lead to work in another, as in this panel in strings and rope based on the study of cross-sections of wood.

An old boat being reconditioned by a middle school boy.

Opposite:
The pattern of wood grain inspired this panel in string and rope (photo Mary Seyd).

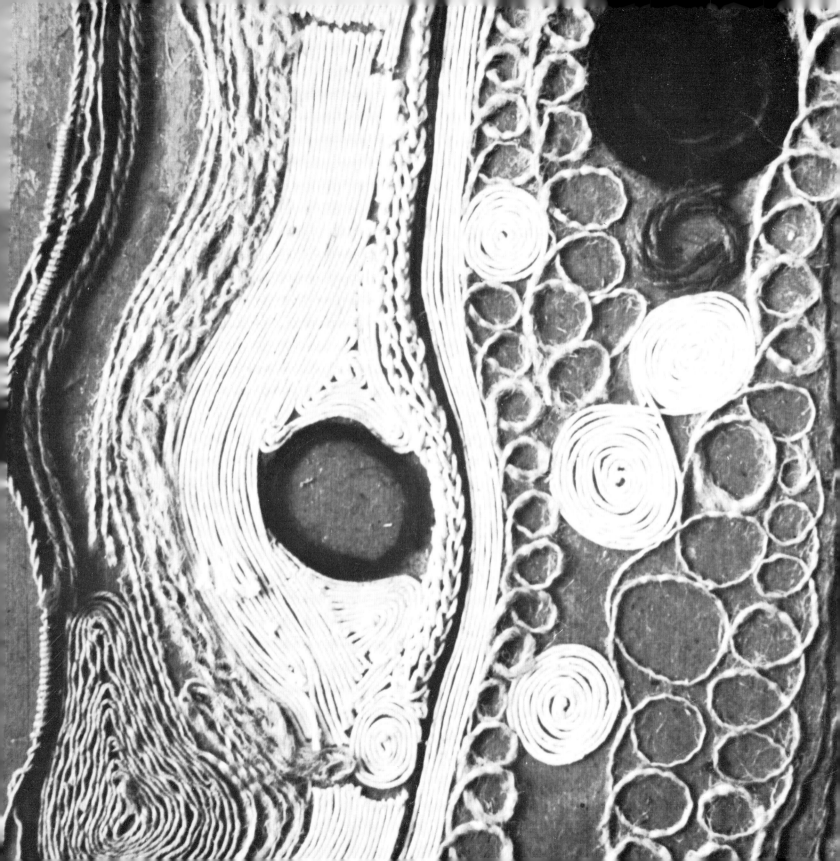

Soft stone, clunch and alabaster come directly from the earth itself. Clunch or soft white limestone, which can be picked up from road works, quarries or chalk cliffs on the seacoast, is soft enough for use by 12 year-old girls. It is found in shapes which themselves suggest ideas and by being turned this way and that will call up the images which seem to lie latent in them. It is a material that by-passes the too common wail of this age group 'I can't draw', and leads the children away from the narrow field of mere representation.

Shapes in waste pieces of alabaster, thrown out from a quarry, can be formed by rasping, filing and polishing. They may be seen simply as shapes, revealing the translucent quality of the material and pleasant to handle, or they may suggest animals or birds, perhaps becoming symbols of the world outside.

All these natural materials remind us of the larger framework of which they are a part. A sycamore seed tells of the cycle of the seasons, leading from bud, flower, winged plane, to future forests; a fossil provides a link with the age before the dinosaurs through the intervening centuries to the marine creatures of our own time.

Sycamore seed (photo Heather Angel).

Opposite:
A girl carving (photo Elizabeth Leyh).

A trilobite fossil provides a link with centuries past.

Chapter 6

ORIGINATING, CREATING

The materials already discussed suggest ideas to us, encouraging us to develop images already latent in them. Henry Moore, for example, has often kept a piece of stone about his studio for years 'waiting for it to tell him what to do with it'. There are materials, such as plants, however, which have for centuries supplied human necessities but do not reveal their properties so directly.

One of the most common products of this type of material is paper, used in every aspect of contemporary life and yet how little of it is interesting as paper. It should provide a tactile pleasure in the ordinary tasks of life, such as making the shopping list, writing letters, even reading reports.

Woad flowers in bloom (photo K. Drummond).

Children will find the simple process of paper-making soothing and stimulating (see page 34); gathering and choosing grasses and straw, finding that different leaves give coloured papers, varying textures and thicknesses. It can be linked with other craft activities; a unique personal paper will add a new quality to a string or lino-print. Lampshades or screens can be made with flower heads, leaves, even wings of butterflies found dead incorporated in the paper, immortalized like a bee in amber.[1]

Dye plants too, are easily accessible to school children. Onion skins are freely available in household waste (see page 30) and gardens or parks offer barks, rotting walnuts and an infinite number of leaves, roots, berries. The flowers of ragwort, tansy, marigold, dahlia, the leaves of lombardy poplar, dog's mercury, lily-of-the-valley, bog myrtle, the berries of bilberry (or whortleberry) and many others, all yield unexpected wealth of colour.

The work of a farmer's wife I visited in East Anglia illustrates the possibilities of using local resources for dyeing. She greeted me dressed in a tweed skirt she had dyed and woven herself, and her isolated farmhouse was rich with chair seats and heavy crocheted floor rugs from her own dyeing. She used the lichens on the barn roof, and the woad leaves (strays from former woad fields) in the ditches which she had guarded from an over-zealous ditcher.

[1] The simple process is described in *Papermaking as an Artistic Craft* by John Mason, Twelve by Eight, 1963.

Lichen growing on a rock, and wools dyed with lichen colours.

Picture of the madder plant from an old herbal (photo CIBA).

Children can sow woad seeds and plant madder cuttings in large window boxes or strips of garden, watch their growth and extract the colour themselves from leaves and roots. For dyeing they will only need a means of heating (a camp cooker will do if domestic science equipment is not available), pails for rinsing and a washing line. Colours from plant dyes have a subtle quality and their range provides an enormous extension on the limited palette of school paints and crayons.

Dyeing with very simple equipment. Lowering white wool into a pan of dye liquor on a primus stove (photo Geoff Newman).

Left:
Peeling onion skins for dye, tying up hanks ready for dyeing, lifting the dyed wool out of the pan (photo Geoff Newman).

Below:
Labelling hanks of wool with a pouched bag for storing (photo Geoff Newman).

Below:
A carry-cushion crocheted in squares dyed with madder, blackberry, indigo and weld (photo John Hunnex).

*Simple first weavings. The
right example is woven on
the principle of the Red
Indian bow loom (photo
Geoff Newman).*

Once the wools have been dyed they can be used in a number of ways. The children may begin by laying strips in a simple weave, on a home-made loom, and can go on to macramé, knitting, crochet, embroidery – so popular now for adolescent garments. In the country, where there is wool waiting to be picked off wire fences, they may combine their dyeing with the rhythmical craft of spinning. Others may tie-dye headscarves, ties, aprons or skirts. The pride of these primary school children in their dyed aprons and ties reflects the excitement of actually making colour. The popular method of tying material anyhow in knots and thrusting it into a dye bath should not be allowed to obscure the real craft of tie-dyeing which requires precise and careful binding or stitching to bring out its full beauty. A length of an Indian sari or an intricate Javanese patterning in rice and seeds show the results of a real command of the medium.

A child's sampler made with fibres all dyed with one plant, the nettle (photo Geoff Newman).

Children in tie-dyed aprons.

Woven hanging made without a loom from plant dyed fibres, reeds and grasses (photo Pennsylvania State University).

Perhaps, building on the earlier instances of string work, some youngsters will enjoy weaving, first without looms (see pages 30 and 35) and building either mathematical structures on nails or pins or in free netlike weaves. Or they may work at discovering combinations of texture which can, at a later age, be incorporated in weavings such as window screens or room dividers, open not solid structures, which echo our understanding of the open structure of matter. Of course, uncovering hidden forms, assembling and arranging, shaping, all move comprehensively into creating in the fullest sense of the word, collaborating with the nature materials.

The historical interest of dyes can also be emphasized. A new dimension will be added for children by stories of the use of woad by the Ancient Britons, of how the trade in indigo and brasilwood sent adventurers to open up the New World, or of how Queen Elizabeth I was so offended by the smell produced by the woad trade in East Anglia that the many beds she slept in mark her attempts to avoid the woad towns.

A young teacher in East Anglia carried out a project linking historical and geographical studies of dyes with practical work. Her 9 year-old class gathered dyes and made collections of samples. They also made a study of the indigo trade with visits to local museums, taking brass-rubbings of the rich merchants' tombs in local churches, and collecting their studies in excellent workbooks. Their drawings recorded traditional dye processes and trade ships, and cloth halls and market places were drawn from observation. At the same time they were dyeing and using their dyes in weaving, knitting and crochet. This type of work with children illustrates the scope of one product of the natural world, and the possibilities of combining a number of natural materials and different crafts to produce an infinite variety of results.

An interest in the wool trade led some children to make brass rubbings in their local church (photo Victoria and Albert Museum, Crown Copyright).

HOW WILL THE TEACHERS GAIN CONFIDENCE?

There is an infinite variety of ways of working with natural materials for children; I have mentioned only a few and have been concerned with suggesting *possibilities* rather than 'how-to-do-it' tips. One of the best opportunities for a teacher to extend his or her knowledge in this field is provided by the craft workshops and short craft courses all over the country, which offer the experience of working craftsmen. There are also evening classes giving the kind of practical teaching that is all too often needed. Failing that, there are now numerous helpful books available, many of which are listed in the bibliography. Once he has made a start with a new material, a teacher can experiment alongside his pupils, learning from their inventiveness and from the material itself to discover new forms.

At every point I have tried to suggest activities which are not childish things to be dropped with contempt at a later stage, not artificial activities confined to a narrow school environment, but experiments which are usually related to traditional crafts. This traditional wisdom is directly linked to the contemporary crafts practised by artist craftsmen in growing numbers. Their work, which can be seen in galleries in major cities and in smaller travelling exhibitions, is an inspiration to us as teachers and to the children.[1]

[1] Exhibitions of crafts are now circulated by many Institutes of Education where school parties can visit them. Museums of local crafts and archaeology are springing up in many counties. Major exhibitions of 'Primitive' and contemporary crafts are organised by the World Craft Council who have also published a beautiful book *Crafts of the Modern World* by Slivka, Webb and Patch. Horizon Press, New York, 1969.

HELPING WITHOUT DESTROYING THE CREATIVE IMPULSE

Creative work arises out of a deep response either to an external object or to an inner impulse. Children are possessed by personal themes which they passionately need to pursue and which can be given form through the medium of words or the materials of the physical world. The teacher is therefore faced with the problem of giving opportunities to many different children to develop their varied responses, which may at one moment involve a search for knowledge and at another, for the images through which the inner life communicates.[1]

His conviction that *this* is his job as a teacher whether he is a general primary teacher or a specialist, should give him priorities which prevent confusion and strain. If he decides in all practice of the arts to give priority to *sustaining the inner life* he has a measure of evaluation for every situation. Techniques are then not ends in themselves but the language through which we speak in order to communicate something we care about.

This conviction about priorities promotes calmness and tolerance in the midst of apparent confusion and

[1] This is most clearly demonstrated in *Study of Imagination in Early Childhood and its Functions in Mental Development* by R. Griffiths, Routledge & Kegan Paul, 1935

the infinite variety of response. But the teacher's organisation, provision of materials, upkeep of tools, storage and retrieval, have to be good enough to enable him and the children to pursue their work without hindrance or waste of time. This is the prerequisite.[1] When groups become at home in that situation (and this argues for spending a fair proportion of time with one teacher if possible, not just meeting him briefly once a week or once a fortnight) then they take responsibility for not only their own work but for their borrowed tools and working space. The teacher is then free to deal with more fundamental individual problems and small emergencies.

If the essence of creativity is discovering or making new things, then the creative teacher must free himself from objectives that are too specific and be ready to accept unexpected happenings. If we ask to share a child's thoughts or invite him to be free to express them, we need to look beyond our own expectations, deeper than any superficial standards, and perceive what is happening below the surface. However, before we can intervene we need to stand back and observe, attaining a degree of detachment: *to know when and where to intervene is the whole delicately balanced art of a teacher.* At times we need to give children courage to try new things, at others we must emphasize the need for pursuing one objective rather than seeking the novelty and escape of constant change. Sometimes we need to encourage the child who doubts the validity of his work and sometimes we need to wait until we know what to say. Sometimes we may have to give the stimulus of excursions into a new environment or new materials, or the leadership in initiating a group experience or celebrating a festival. Always we must be prepared to allow children *time* to bring their ideas to fruition, without expecting too much from them too soon. Contact with natural materials can reinforce this attitude in us, as we develop our awareness of the gradual growth of all living things, whether they be plants, birds, animals or children. Even in the death of a bird or the felling of a tree there are new beginnings, new inspirations, inexhaustible meanings.

[1] See Appendix on Art and the Education of Teachers in *Children's Growth through Creative Experience*. Van Nostrand Reinhold, 1974.

PERSONAL RESPONSES MAY BE THE STARTING POINT FOR MANY DIFFERENT EXPERIENCES

Two examples

The response to a bird's skeleton

This is a found object which can be brought into the school.

The response to the cut trunk of a tree

This could be seen in the playground or on an excursion into the countryside.

Investigation focused on a specific problem

A study of why the proportion of wing span to body cavity expresses the height and duration of flight.

A study of this tree, its history and its age in rings, its life cycle and uses.

A lateral investigation widening out to adjacent fields

How do birds' skeletons differ from and how resemble those of reptiles and mammals?
How did this bird, when living, feed, mate and build? Why does it have this type of beak, these particular claws?

What is the place of trees in ecology?
How do they renew our atmosphere?
What creatures do they shelter?

Representational studies can develop from appreciation of a chosen object

Studies for the portrayal of a bird's plumage, noting whether it is for display or protection.
Studies of the flight and nesting habits of birds.

Studies of the individual structure of the species, as displayed in winter, and of the seating of woods in our landscape.
Studies of the ancient gnarled giant outliving many generations.

Or a piece of craftwork can be made from it or incorporate it

The skeleton might be incorporated in a structure of wires, which would emphasize its fragility and imprisonment.

A piece of wood might be carved into a sculpture displaying its qualities, or gouged into a bowl or spoon, warm and sympathetic to the hand.

Or it might serve as the theme of a festival or dance

A dance based on the different characters of birds, with their various movements and cries, using head-dresses and costumes.

A festival of trees in which seeds are planted indoors, or woods and road verges planted with saplings. When camping the tree can be made the basis for totem rites.

Bibliography

NATURAL MATERIALS

Bjorn A.	Exploring Fire and Clay	Van Nostrand Reinhold, New York and London, 1970
Blumeneau, L.	Creative Design in Wall Hangings	George Allen & Unwin, London, 1968
Coker, A.	Craft of Straw Decoration	Dryad, London, 1971
Hils, K.	Crafts for All	Routledge & Kegan Paul, London and Boston, 1960
Hutton, H.	Mosaic Making	Batsford, London, 1966
Maile, A.	Tie and Dye as a Present Day Craft	Mills & Boon, London, 1967
Mason, J.	Papermaking as an Artistic Craft	Twelve by Eight, Leicester, 1963
Newick, J.	Clay and Terracotta in Education	Dryad, London, 1964
Parker, C.	Inspiration for Embroidery	Batsford, London, 1967
Petrie, M.	Modelling	Dryad, London, 1964
Rainey, S.	Weaving without a Loom	Davis, Massachusetts, 1966
Robertson, S. M.	Beginning at the Beginning with Clay	Society for Education through Art, London, 1965
Robertson, S. M.	Creative Crafts in Education	Routledge & Kegan Paul, London and Boston, 1952
Seyd, M.	Designing with String	Batsford, London, 1967
Seyd, M.	Introducing Beads	Batsford, London, 1973
Waters, D. and Rutter O.	Creative Work with Found Materials	Mills & Boon, London, 1971
Wright, B.	Baskets and Basketry	Batsford, London, 1959

FURTHER READING

Leach, B.	Potter's Book	Faber and Faber, London, 1945
Lowenfeld, V.	The Nature of Creative Activity	Routledge & Kegan Paul, London and Boston, 1939 (first edition)
Richards, E.	In the Early World	New Zealand Council for Education Research, Wellington, 1964
Robertson, S. M.	Dyes from Plants	Van Nostrand Reinhold, New York and London, 1973
Robertson, S. M.	Rosegarden and Labyrinth	Routledge & Kegan Paul, London and Boston, 1963
Wachowiak, F.	Emphasis; Art	International Textbook, 1971
Zechlin, R.	Complete Book of Handicrafts	Branford, Massachusetts, 1968